K.P. ALEXANDER

A Raven in the Snow

First published by K.P. Alexander 2024

Copyright © 2024 by K.P. Alexander

All rights reserved. No part of this publication may be reproduced, stored or transmitted in any form or by any means, electronic, mechanical, photocopying, recording, scanning, or otherwise without written permission from the publisher. It is illegal to copy this book, post it to a website, or distribute it by any other means without permission.

First edition

ISBN (paperback): 978-1-7387380-3-8
ISBN (hardcover): 978-1-7387380-4-5

This book was professionally typeset on Reedsy.
Find out more at reedsy.com

To my eternal muse,
May you find yourself in these pages
And think of me...

Contents

Preface vi
Prologue viii

I THE COLD OF A SINGING SLEEP

PURGATORY'S WHISPER ECHOS ON	3
A TEMPER RAGES AGAINST INNOCENCE	4
ANCESTRAL ACCESSORIES WORN BY MANY	5
THE GREAT GARDEN	6
UNSPOKEN GRIEF	8
FAITHLESS FANTASIES LEFT TO ROT	10
THE COWARD'S ACT	12
KILLING INNOCENCE WITH A SHARPENED HAND	14
A SLUMBERING MADNESS	15
THE POISONED ACT	16
LASTING MEMORIES OF COURT	18
BEING RAISED IN WAR'S NAME	19
THE FINE LINES OF YOUTH	20
THE CRY OF LIFE	21
THE FEELING OF RAIN	23
PREMONITIONS OF YOUTH	25
DESTINY'S INFERNO	27
WINGS MAY COME	29
THE FORCE OF WILL	30

SPARK OF THE SOUL	32
WADING IN	33
EXISTENCE BECOMES IN BELIEF	34
THE PEACE IN EACH BREATH	35
HAPPINESS REVEALED	36
THE SORROW JAR	38
LICKING THE LAST OF ESSENCE FROM A DROP	39
PHANTOMS THAT CARESS THE SKIN	40
ASHES TO ASHES, I BECOME FROM DUST	42
THE GRIP OF THE PEN	44
A POET'S GUILT	45
THE MAD(CREATIVITY)NESS	46
A VICTOR'S WALK AMONGST THE WILLOWS	47
I WILL FOLLOW THAT GREAT FLOWER	49
A COLLECTION OF THOUGHTS AT MIDNIGHT	51
AN UNEXPECTED EMBRACE	52
I MAKE A PROMISE WITH INFINITY	53

II   THE PATH OF AFFECTION'S FAVOUR

YOUTHFUL JESTS	57
WHAT WAS LEFT AT BREAK OF DAY	58
THE CLOVER'S ABSENT KISS	59
AFFECTION'S GUARD	61
LOVE'S LEAST FAVOURITE INHERITANCE	62
A HEIGHT TOO FAR FOR ME	63
DEPRIVATION IS A DREAMER	64
THE INDULGENCE OF A MOMENT TAKEN FOR GRANTED	65
LOVE'S JESTER	66
THE WISH YOU CRY	67

AN IMPOSTER CREEPING UPON THE LIGHT OF DAY	68
WHEN A FLAME MET THE WIND	71
THE NOTES THAT CARRY	73
AT YOUR FEET	75
TWO OF CUPS	77
AN AUTUMN WIND'S DREAMING	79
THE HAUNTING THAT HOLDS ME	80
A FLOWER GROWS FROM A BROKEN STONE	81
THE BROKEN PIECES FIT	83
THE VOW THAT GUIDES US HOME	84
THE POETRY OF THE DARK'S DEPTH	86
THE MISTRESS	88
A WRINKLE IN TIME	89
WHEN RUINS TURNED BACK INTO PALACES	91
WHERE WE FALL	93
THE LAST PETALS OF LOVE'S REGRET	94
PHANTOM PAINS	96
THE GHOSTS THAT VISIT THE DEAD	97
AFTER	98
LOVE'S REMEMBRANCE	100
WHAT MELODY KNEW OF US	101
OLD SOULS TETHERED TO THE WAKING	103
THE PEACE IN REST	105
THE CONSTELLATION OF OUR NAME	106

III   THE FLIGHT OF WISDOM'S NAME

THE QUESTIONS ASKED BETWEEN CRADLE AND GRAVE	111
TRAGEDY'S HYPNOSIS	112

TO LIVE PAST MEMORY	113
HEIRLOOMS	115
WHAT BECAME OF AN OPENED DOOR	116
THE GIFT OF TIME	117
A SEANCE OF MY SETTLED SELF	119
JUST A WHISPER	120
THE SANDGLASS WHISPERS	122
THE NAKEDNESS OF YOUR FAVOURITE THOUGHT	123
THE GENTLEST OF NIGHTTIME FANCIES	124
A PAST LIFE LAID TO REST	126
THE CONSTELLATIONS OF MY SKIN	128
THE SILK OF SALVATION	130
A CALLING BLESSED	131
LEGEND'S FIRST AND LAST LAUGH	132
A TESTAMENT TO SOUL	134
SIN'S ALLURE	135
APPETITE	137
THE EDGE	138
THE PURITY OF LOVE-DRIVEN NECROMANCY	139
RISING WITH A HERO'S NAME	141
UNWRITTEN SANCTUARIES	143
FIREWORKS	144
ONE MOMENT LIVING IN TIME TWICE	146
ANTIQUE BOOKS	147
MY DEVOTION	149
A CELESTIAL PERSPECTIVE	150
VERITAS	152
A MIDNIGHT VISITOR	153
A FAREWELL	155
AUTUMN'S WELCOME	157
THE BREATHING PERHAPS	158

WHAT WHISPERS ON A MEADOW GREEN	160
A REMEMBRANCE WAITING	162
THE KEY IS FOUND IN HISTORY	163
WHISPERS ON THE WIND	165
Epilogue	167
Acknowledgments	169
About the Author	171

Preface

A truth exists, hidden within these pages, woven through every line of speech made simple and every rhyme held by the mysticism of nurtured thought; a certain possession of self that compelled me to articulate what I know of a lost century's last breath; this grandness of being oneself and another through one word twice said; with you, I share this *nostos* for tasting a lost thing on your tongue through the poetry I have written in Existence's name.

What I have given, that which was carelessly left and placed carefully, belongs to me;

What is found- *loved, hated, remembered, or forgotten*- within these pages, upon being read, belongs to you;

The characters of this poetry are spectres and spectators of your life, as well as mine; they do not belong to me, but I have written of them, and through this, they will perhaps make themselves known to you- in strange or familiar ways.

Existence is but a moment, the living and the dying. The Dreaming Awake is ours to decorate- with light, with touch- and perhaps, in another century, there will be a stillness, a golden softness for the souls who greet it, and what will be remembered of us is that we loved with art, found breath in song, knew the Divine through the beauty shared of ourselves- expressions of creativity honouring Truth and Time- and because of it all, we lived and were *alive*.

Prologue

Looking at the freshly fallen snow,
   It's cold,
   But there is something so warming
   In the tended quiet of a street, undisturbed.
   A raven sits atop the gently settled snow,
   So defined by the shock of its blessed feathers.
   It calls out, only an echo returning its ancient plea.

What is in a raven's call?
   A warning? A message? For you?
   The raven screams, but is there anyone left to hear it?
   Does anyone listen to this raven's call?

There is a silent solitude that slithers amongst the Undisturbed,
   As soft and Unbecoming as the veil of snow
   On a street made voiceless.

Amidst the shades of the Unceasing,
   Sits an outlier, an opponent to the Undisturbed.
   This obsidian Other,
   As sharp and Unconforming as the scream that leaves its body,
   Calls out to the cold,
   Calls out to the quiet,
   Calls out...

Is it an echo that returns its plea?
   Is it a plea that has echoed in kinship?
   What is in *this* call?
   Is there anyone left in the silence to return the message?

When the commands of Destiny reach out,
   With obsidian claws and piercing wails,
   Will you remain silent at Solitude's side?
   Or will you reach back,
   With shaking hands and a hoarse voice,
   To become,
   To speak,
   To be one of the Unconquered?

A raven does not call as a compulsion of nature...it calls to be heard.

I

THE COLD OF A SINGING SLEEP

PURGATORY'S WHISPER ECHOS ON

It's the break of the beautiful that writes tragedy,
   Etches devastation onto the bones
   Of the broken, wasted, and delusional;
   Lungs that heave with tainted breath
   Find a sweetness left from crushed petals
   Of a corrupted flower;
   There is a thrill woven into the wind,
   A sense of unnatural wonder in the flight
   Of a fall;
   Such are the echoes of the In-Between:
   Impressions of Song twisted by hollowness and the mockery
   Of an empty, unreturned call…

A TEMPER RAGES AGAINST INNOCENCE

Violet skies,
   With their serenity and mockery,
   Break with every silent sob of the unpardonable Innocent;

Faultless tears turn to blood,
   Breaking promises against the soft melancholy of an unbroken heart;

Troubled minds turn bodies into infernal creatures,
   And Serenity falls beneath Mockery's hand,
   As skies turn violent with the wrath of the Patient and the Cunning…

ANCESTRAL ACCESSORIES WORN BY MANY

We deliver the ghosts of our pain and sadness
   Under the stormy sky of the Unfulfilled
   As a consequence of our cowardice.

We are the craven parents to bastard children whose own journeys become tainted
   By the unaccomplished of our own;
   Their pain is not theirs,
   Their sorrow does not belong to them,
   But to them, they have been given,
   To suppress,
   In the hope that our ignorance will cure
   What demands to be known.

THE GREAT GARDEN

The sweetness of a scar severs us from the kindness
    That we so freely give to serpents who steal
    The beauty of simple things,
    (The bravery won and lost in every war,
    Or a long lost love's last wish on their North star),
    These things, serpents steal with the beauty robbed
    From the Kindly,
    Those too dear in mind,
    In suffering,
    To be held above or below
    Those who would befriend Ignorance
    In place of their elusion of Fear.

To scare where one would love!

They simply wish,
    The Kindly,
    To desire something that they feel worthy of,
    But it's not their place to stake a claim
    On something that the serpents love
    To ruin, taint, trick, and shame.

The villainy is in the very act,
   Not of deceiving,
   But of ruining the beauty of a simple thing
   That once belonged to a pure heart
   Who fell beneath the serpents' ire
   And found suffering in the same place
   Where they should have been loved
   And found in their desires.

UNSPOKEN GRIEF

Unspoken Grief,
    Misery's favourite and most laborious child,
    Is adopted by the Unquiet.

It settles in between the mists of the Aged
    And the hollowed caverns in the heart of the Abandoned.

Here,
    In this unhappy house,
    (Though happiness would not make it home),
    The salty waters run as clear
    As the taint that has let them go;
    To bleed is to be lost,
    As air escapes,
    As air *punishes*,
    Leaving a darkness for the wounded,
    A darkness for the forever left behind.

A bedtime story is told,
    Desperate in its expression,
    Vivid in its belief,
    And Hope begins the tale on every night,

Radiant in its song,
Light in its touch,
But to this end, there is no relief,
For Misery holds the story now,
And the ending has been written by
Unspoken Grief.

FAITHLESS FANTASIES LEFT TO ROT

I am the severed fragments of shattered Expectation.

So sudden came the blow,
   (Unexpected for me,
   One who had known only warmth and fullness, alone),
   I am a severed thing now, separate but warm still.
   A piece of me remains with the fracture born
   From the attentions of unreturned affection,
   The other belongs to the breaking wrought
   By the unlikely hands of my own will.

An assaulted thing finding fate
   In a purgatory for the lost and never found,
   I have come to know that the price of one's happiness
   Is the presence of another's.
   I stood no chance against the ambitions of unsatiated Simplicity,
   And now I am left unburied, restless above ground.

There can be no understanding in our individuality,
   Nor hope for our souls' desires,
   When we are tethered to the belief
   That the freedom of one robs the liberation of all;

I knew little of comfort before I was slain,
Now, in pieces, I am forced to love sudden, unhappy Grief.

Why must the chains always be worn?
    I am tired of games that require a violent end!
    I was alive for a time, but I did not stay.
    I am a severed thing now,
    For I could not see the hidden foe in a most beloved friend
    When shattered Expectation, *unfortunately*, came my way.

THE COWARD'S ACT

To perform is to write
    The damning thoughts across the stage
    Of this expressionless, accepting page;
    Carried through the glide of every word,
    A dreamer finds sanctuary in delusion,
    An illusion of their own design…

But there persists a thought,
    A wonder really,
    If sanctuary *without* can truly be such
    If solace *within* does not first exist.
    In dreams, they feel what they dared to imagine,
    A vision they believed into being,
    A hope they had sold to Cowardice.

Desire then rests
    In the disquiet of Coward's design,
    And in the forsaken chains forged
    By unshaken Insecurity,
    Desire forms a dream of its own:

To manifest as life,

THE COWARD'S ACT

To be true in its form
As it had been true in thought…
Not to exist as a phantom of possibility,
Desolate and trapped,
Following faithfully to the end,
Performing the final show,
(For performing is all it ever was),
Committing to the Coward's greatest and final act.

KILLING INNOCENCE WITH A SHARPENED HAND

Forgotten were the words said
   By a malice so pure;
   Remembered were the words heard
   By the obsession of Malice's taint,
   A vulnerable so bright, unsteady,
   And terribly unsure.

It was Wickedness that raised its hand,
   But it was sad Acquiescence that accepted it.
   What was gifted in the shadows
   Was still a gift in the light of day,
   (A bitter taste to know),
   Too shocking to understand
   That a gift may be a gift still
   In eager hands and sparkling eyes.
   It's Prayer's vulnerability,
   Pleading in quiet, with its own desperate hand,
   May this gift be a gift!
   (Though it was gifted to break bones
   And assail what remains of an ignorant, naive will).

A SLUMBERING MADNESS

Exhaustion overtakes the nightmare
   Of some spiteful dreamer's dream;
   Untouchable in waking,
   It is not touch nor taste that claims the name
   Of this frightened nightmare,
   Nor can it be seen when the warmth of day chases away
   The coldness nursed by ignorant Sleep, entirely just and unfair.
   This spectre belongs to Thought alone.
   For it is easier to hate a nightmare in its unpunishable anger
   Than it is to love the sadness of a recurring dream
   Made of bitter agony and brittle, breakable bone.

THE POISONED ACT

What belongs to the performative villain,
   Alone on that borrowed, grim stage,
   With his broken lines of speech,
   Unrehearsed and unpleasantly strange?

It is not the dagger,
   Frightening, and flourishing, and unbelonging to those practiced hands,
   That bears the name of villainy,
   Nor is it the poison made of watered wine and artistic skill
   That makes a villain of his forced company.

A classically trained leech of the gallery's design,
   Sucking the tainted life from every seat,
   Growing fat and swollen through his expected gluttony,
   Absolving through a doomed pantomime,
   This villain is just an empty spectre to these vicious spectators.

For what is seen in the audience's joined stare?
   Ah, that is the gift our performative villain has been forced to bear!
   The true villainy belongs to those who watch,
   Those who mimic Virtue in their finest,

And the only true possession belonging to our poor villain
Is the knowledge possessing him,
The truth of true villainy,
A fact forgotten in his condemned villain's silenced care.

LASTING MEMORIES OF COURT

There is no venom in a vicious word spoken by others
   If you have spoken the same one to yourself;
   If you have swallowed venom for delight
   And spit it at wavering reflections in mirrored cages,
   Then there is no surprise by which you can ever be taken;
   To wait for the poison would be a foolish game
   For the the people's favourite fool,
   But to prepare the drink of the last move,
   To tip it back, and rewrite the Game of Fools,
   Then you will hold a master's cup
   Over the heads of the ignorantly thirsty,
   The unnecessarily cruel,
   And you will escape the very game they promised,
   The very game they forgot how to win,
   The game into which they themselves have been foolishly lured.

BEING RAISED IN WAR'S NAME

A weapon of mass destruction:
   A soul woven with the delicate threads of grace
   And the violent shards of ever-waiting anarchy;
   It hovers between the safety of Never-Becoming
   And the ruins of Ordinary Remembrance.

This is a promised war,
   For this life or the next,
   And the bloody hand that takes the palm of Peace
   Will only find it when the unscathed other
   Chooses the hand of Chaos.

THE FINE LINES OF YOUTH

What is in the waters of Youth
   That makes us feel so old?

Before we truly learn how to breathe,
   Something settles in our marrow
   And calls out to the sweet release
   Of chaos;
   We are introduced to Age before we even reach it
   And find that the greyness of life comes paired
   With the colours of the world.

We rest in the afternoons of our everyday
   Before true wakefulness takes our hands,
   And when a cataracts replaces our sight
   Before we even see the morning,
   We lose the truth that Youth bestows
   As a parting gift:

Life is the healer that wreaks ruin,
   And there is pleasure in this pain,
   But humanity has always been too alive
   To crave the end that comes too soon.

THE CRY OF LIFE

I reject Youth because I do not know when it begins
   Or when it comes to an end;
   The sweet breath of gentle childhood
   Is just a breath's length in being
   Until the sharpness of Sight settles upon
   The joined hands of Responsibility and Freedom.

It is often in a single moment that one
   Inhales a tender breath to find that it returns to the world bitter;
   Just as often, in another,
   Tenderness makes ready the eager lungs,
   Accustomed to the Untainted and Undisturbed,
   So that one never really knows when Tenderness quietly steps away
   And is replaced by something heavier,
   Something much greater.

Within Youth and without,
   I find myself.
   There are chains upon my joviality
   But an inexplicable lightness in all that I carry.

Perhaps it is not Youth I reject,

(For perhaps that has never been its name),
I think Life is what I know,
And it is Life that I will *one day* come to love.

THE FEELING OF RAIN

I like the rain.

A soft smile touches my lips
   With the raw admission that passes through yours.

You're speaking in codes,
   The codes of Despair,
   And, *darling*, I speak them well.

We like the rain.

We have been touched by Darkness,
   And so the rain touches us in ways
   That only the lonely can feel.
   Each drop of favoured memory
   Falls to the ground in perfect time
   With the constant rhythm
   Of our sacred salt.

Though the shadows may dance with us,
   We choose to dance with them in the rain.

We are held by trauma
   But are embraced by memory.

We like the rain.

The causal way that you speak
   Of your vulnerabilities
   Says more than your careful words.

We're bound together,
   You and I,
   By the darkness that touches our souls
   And the drops of water that kiss our skin.

I like the rain, too.

PREMONITIONS OF YOUTH

Where along this path of ours
    Did we become all of the things
    We said we would never become?

What beautiful liars we all are!
    Such delightful fools
    To believe that we could become anything more
    Than our greatest fears!

In fright, we tethered our Becoming
    To the very things we prayed would never come to life,
    And now we're frighteningly alive,
    Living in the shadows of our greatest enemies,
    Casting the same spectres that once held our fear.

We devoured our pain to see it gone,
    But as we grew in Age,
    It grew in Patience,
    Waiting for the day when we had gone,
    Moved forward in life,
    So that it could devour,
    So that we could never truly move on.

In the absence of our faith,
   We Became in our fear,
   And now, for our lives,
   As we became,
   So, too, must we be undone.

DESTINY'S INFERNO

In a flame, with embers stoked in Hope and Rage,
   I found what was left to me of a broken name;
   Dangers that promised,
   Kissed,
   With the light of something warm.
   Undisciplined in the burning,
   But exquisite when made tame,
   I saw Destiny shining back at me
   In a light that saw me screaming.

I sat with these flames,
   So satisfied in the knowing that I could burn
   If I chose to stay.
   What an end it would be,
   To be worshipped by something,
   To feel alive before I was left
   Where I had been laid, faithfully, to rest;
   To pray with the smoke that took hymns
   From the sweat on my brow!

Oh, but it was to a single dance
   Alone

That I gave my company!
Though it was a joy to be remembered,
Responsibility was the one to make me bow
In the end,
To settle me with Duty,
To make me see that all I loved would burn forever
Under the wrath of the one flame who held me,
Gently.

An inferno's gift and greatest guise
   Was to grant me the promise of a different life,
   To polish the ashes that fell from my eyes;
   It is here, between blaze and blame,
   That I would rest myself
   Should Choice favour me again.
   I left the flames that had stoked me silent,
   But they sit inside the mind
   They could not burn.
   I left Hope and Rage,
   (I will remember in the same moment they yearn,
   But still, I left),
   And the flames devoured what remained
   Of my first and only dance
   And my once-broken name.

WINGS MAY COME

Wings may carry me through a flight,
   (Forsaken this once not to fall),
   And I may be the majesty of soaring gales
   In the mildness of a limber night;

May Descent claim another
   And wings carry what I cannot
   Along a way that knew me well
   At the last earnest call of my first creative thought;

Let this flight carry my belief
   That one may soar and not know ruin,
   That one may fly beyond fleeting Insanity
   And have their faith be grounded;
   To be a dream's favourite dream,
   And for once, finally know
   What it is for wings to carry me.

THE FORCE OF WILL

To Doom, I was born.
    A spiral of Strength's design,
    It was in this force of fight or flight
    That I chose to find indulgence in both
    The chase of fear and the battle against it.

Introduced to no one along the way
    But my own glory and dwindling shame,
    I discovered a compulsion towards an
    Everlasting peace born from the shock of life
    And debilitating pain.

The hand that reached out to rescue
    The Whimpering and Afraid
    Belonged to the same body that bore
    Strength's name;

I held that trembling hand.
    That hand reached out from an almost-certain me.

From the chaos of this birth
    Began the roots from which my light stemmed,

And I was frightened for a time
When shadows mimicked my every move,
But to Doom, I was not condemned,
For I was born *alive*.

SPARK OF THE SOUL

It was just a moment,
   The Spark that introduced me to my life,
   Rosy tint and golden gleam,
   The great Warmth of lovers dearly held,
   Found, lost, and known again,
   After Ego's reign of fright and strife
   Gave way for the spring of Rest
   Under the sheltering of a waiting evergreen.

Alight,
   I am loved.
   Fumbled, fallen, but unafraid,
   May my death be merciless,
   Let Terror make a saviour out of me,
   For it was in just one moment
   That a spark came forth to astonish,
   To breathe,
   To lay bare all that I was meant to be.

WADING IN

The numbing shock of life:
   A stark reminder that I exist!
   In these moments,
   Frozen,
   Paralyzed,
   I recognize that I am alive.

It is the remembrance of warmth,
   The presence of unending coldness,
   That feeds me the thrill of my mortality.

I exist hopelessly on the precipice
   Of waters too shallow to hold me
   And depths that vow to swallow me whole.

EXISTENCE BECOMES IN BELIEF

The *nothing* that consumes your greater thoughts
   Of what you are,
   Of what Destiny brought you to be,
   Is a fantasy written by slithering spectres
   In the wakefulness of a poisoned dream.

The *everything* that looms behind the wispy glass
   Of your nurtured forgetfulness
   Is exquisite being of Delight's design;
   It is here that truth begins,
   This sacred place of remembering that you are living
   To be alive.

THE PEACE IN EACH BREATH

This life,
   In splendour and in sorrow,
   Was the very affair that my soul needed…

Liberation's transience inspired Song,
   Made breath for essence,
   And tenderly, I knew that I was living to be alive.

I have fallen in love with this promise of life,
   And so Life has given me the promise of purpose.

HAPPINESS REVEALED

This distraction of the Unfulfilled's design
    Enslaves the *happiest* of our greatest minds,
    And the taint of this sin,
    Of this apathetic essence,
    Paralyzes the senses and
    Condemns the integrity of
    Honest labour.

When found with Happiness alone,
    So fragile a being one becomes through
    This unfaithful friend,
    And so a purgatory is built
    For the victims of the Unfulfilled,
    A seemingly endless end.

Happiness slips through the cracks
    Of well-built destruction,
    Leaving prisoners of Pain,
    The Deceived and Undetermined,
    The perfect prey for united Doubt
    And divided Blame.

HAPPINESS REVEALED

It was Happiness that you had,
    But it was not Happiness that you truly sought,
    For in the depths of your great Becoming,
    It was Contentment that you craved,
    It was Purpose that you adored,
    And through their sturdy hands,
    You rose,
    And now you crave no more.

THE SORROW JAR

Sorrow's sleep is restlessness in the careful quiet
   Of lovely things that Time taught me to miss;
   Crystal rings of sacred salt,
   (Once worn and devotedly blessed
   By the remembered hands of
   Horror, Honour, and Happiness),
   Were forgotten when sealing what was left of my darkly beloved,
   Reminiscence.
   Shut once and kissed twice,
   It was with the promise of a savoured life
   That Sorrow found its peace
   In a crystal palace that made sacred
   The salt of its eternal rest.

LICKING THE LAST OF ESSENCE FROM A DROP

In this vial of coveted hope,
   Stars reflect being within depths of inky blue,
   They shimmer within that shallow glass,
   (It is nothing more than all I have:
   What I love and what I have grown to wholly detest).
   It has remained as something ancient, something new,
   And I see that it is here that my fate has finally come to rest.

To float within the current
   Of waters turned infinite and impure,
   To shine as brightness, goodness, and loveliness,
   The very best of the weakest,
   The greatest of those who must endure,
   I meet Fate in this final place
   To take what is left of all that remains to me:
   This vial of hope sustained,
   The cunning poison and the heavenly cure.

PHANTOMS THAT CARESS THE SKIN

Vicarious agony broke in me
   What would not fall to Circumstance.
   I lived through the bruising of so soft a vein
   To find myself singing along to Grief's great lullaby.
   (It was a small dream to think that in the Scathing
   Such softness would be left to survive).

Strength did not leave me at this chance
   Of too many lessons to be learned,
   But it came to me differently,
   Wore the softness of my broken vein with shyness,
   (It steadied my breath with a whispering touch).

Numbness was won in this,
   (To feel nothing at all is still something to feel
   When you have nothing left but the breath
   To yearn),
   And then it was not alone in the possession of a breaking thing,
   For Softness was summoned and returned to me,
   In victory,
   And agony returned to being felt,
   If felt at all,

Vicariously.

ASHES TO ASHES, I BECOME FROM DUST

Destiny is a fire that sees to the burning
   Of many a name,
   Behesting Will to summon a blaze,
   The burning,
   Sacrificing thought and rest
   To hold the villainous heat with the same grasp
   That flowers a flame.

The burning,
   I rise as smoke in choking grace,
   And I settle as ash,
   I tame as light,
   Afraid of Shadow and devoured by Sight;
   I reach the sky as I burn beneath
   Every kindling of pleasure fed,
   Knowledge won,
   And love I did not seek.

I flicker, I wane,
   With Memory keeping me warm
   On Ember's eve,

Pleading to the night for some remembrance
That I did burn,
That I did dance, once, on many a life,
That the burning was a blaze
Of touch and name,
Not just a warm fantasy once tethered
To my belief.

THE GRIP OF THE PEN

To feed to the Passionate,
   To awaken the Uninspired,
   To take up arms against Life
   And offer Truth in its rawest form,
   To reveal Candour in its most biased expression,
   That is the art of broken-hearted poets.

They take what remains of their weariness,
   (*Though they call it their souls*),
   And write an understanding for those who dare to read it
   In the hopes of saving a life
   With the last wisps of their own.

A POET'S GUILT

There is no word too light nor too dark
   For the soul in Wonder.
   To find purpose in it all
   Is the greatest ally,
   To find meaning is to be united.

We walk together and die apart
   Between the life and death
   Of a single word.

...And so that word, we must choose wisely.

THE MAD(CREATIVITY)NESS

My sanity causes chaos in the disturbed thoughts
   That find solace through the guiding hand of Insanity.

The crafted cage of Calmness is Stability's revenge
   For the anarchy that runs wild with Inspiration.

The constant ruination of my soul
   Is embraced, dearly, by the salvation of my heart,
   And they fall and rise with the beautiful precarity of a creative mind.

I breathe and cry,
   Putting myself forward and standing to the side,
   While trying to meet my Madness in meaning,
   To give it purpose so that I may keep what was given to me
   Of life.

A VICTOR'S WALK AMONGST THE WILLOWS

I slaughtered Horror with the kindness
   Promised to me by Sanctuary.

What was given to an innocent thing
   Was carried through as Victory's
   Unpolished, precious jewel,
   And unmarked graves robbed by Strife
   Found a name in the poems written
   To honour their forgotten claim;
   What decayed from that savage fall
   I took for the Wounded,
   (It was them, alone, who sheltered me),
   For there was something to be made
   From what was left of
   The brilliance ravaged, kept, and bloodied.

Life's cemetery calls for me by name;
   I know the guests who stay under the willows,
   There,
   That the weeping echoes in place of voices
   Still remembered by those who remain

Beyond the gates of where
A good birth and tragic death
Have been forged in stony frame.

Horror was in command of the Screaming,
    But it died for a silent song learning to be sung,
    And I stand still.
    I stand listening.
    I stand.

I WILL FOLLOW THAT GREAT FLOWER

It's on Destiny's day,
   At that last hour lost,
   That we hear Hope saying,
   "I will guard your strength with the last of my own,"
   And we hold to that great effort,
   Onwards, always,
   A promise that we will be more
   Than what we became to survive.

All for the sake of someone's love and another's lore,
   But at the end of *my* life,
   It will be *my* story told
   To those saintly fables on another night or day,
   (There is only Time in this light,
   More than the time that we have known,
   And Light has always been the one to stay).

It will be me who sends the fallen feathers
   To my own grave along bitter winds
   That hold echoes of those ghoulish tremors
   Born to laughter,
   And I will find Hope in another time

And be the one to say,
"Strength came and went,
But in you, I found a touch of something great,
Not a glance at Life, but a whisper of the Divine.
Take my hand, now, and I will give you breath,
Again,
With each and every one of mine."

A COLLECTION OF THOUGHTS AT MIDNIGHT

It is on this ruthless night when Mercy finds me,
   Disquiet slipping away as the calmness of rest
   Holds me in my wonder;
   Peace has relieved a life-weary Anarchy,
   And the carnage wrought
   Has laid the silks and satins of Sanctuary at calloused feet.

A hush has befallen this time of mine,
   And I have settled my soul
   In the quiet forgiveness of surrender
   And in the slumbering shadows,
   Now reposed and resigned.

AN UNEXPECTED EMBRACE

In the chaos of Being,
   In the silence of Rest,
   Solitude sat with me and settled its head.

I understood all that it had to say,
   And in kinship,
   It saw all that I was.

So soft and so still in its affection,
   I found light between our clasped hands,
   A supplication woven
   By the audacity of Horror
   And the kindness of Prayer;
   It was a manifestation of a beloved vision,
   My last hope met with the last of despair.

The sweet end to a bitter beginning has held the greatest grace
   In the smallest act,
   And I remain to be forever undone,
   I exist to forever become.

I MAKE A PROMISE WITH INFINITY

The wicked clouds, a sin against the light;
   I could not remember what broke beneath
   The tender savagery of that unholy night,
   But I fell in a fatal dive,
   And Paradise, still gleaming,
   Descended by my side.

I wondered, then, what could be alive,
   After so sudden a death as the Great Depart
   From the carved bone of a kindled-flame sky,
   Alight,
   But I learned that there is nothing so sudden
   As the lushness of a seed's first breath as something green,
   Something born from the earth that took the weight
   Of a fallen thing.

Oh, Beauty! Oh, Grace!
   Let the dew of a morning's first cry
   Bless what fell too far to know the peace
   Of a holy wake and the last dreamer's
   First sigh of faith.

A RAVEN IN THE SNOW

Heaven, lay me bare! Set me free,
   And I will make to you my promise of infinity.

II

THE PATH OF AFFECTION'S FAVOUR

YOUTHFUL JESTS

The softness of Youth's first love:

Each soul consumed by the vastness of a *maybe,*
   Amusing each other with the hidden thought
   Of falling in love,
   A joke for the sake of innocent Affection,
   But within each labouring heart,
   So full of bloom,
   (Not yet touched by the latent ache
   Of fantasy's end,
   Where Age waits as a looming figure),
   They were already
   Madly,
   Deeply,
   Hopefully
   In love.

WHAT WAS LEFT AT BREAK OF DAY

You have compared my happiness to yours,
   And so we see these tiny, stunted seeds sown
   By deliberate Dissonance.
   Undiluted joy has bestowed upon you
   An unsettling of the soul and a break in conscience,
   But where was I to stand in this resentment
   That only you had come to know?

We were partners in this life!
   Happy were *our* hands that,
   Together,
   We were destined to hold,
   But you have found competition in the happy notes
   That we once began to play,
   And now I hold another's hand no more,
   For yours has become unreachable and cold.

THE CLOVER'S ABSENT KISS

To find the end of Faith
    In the paralysis of a soul with no strength left
    To welcome breath into its ethereal lungs.
    The voices of Melody and Hope are now wisps,
    Slowly disappearing;
    Clovers blossomed once when the echoes of love unheard
    Fell upon the fertile soil of promised peace…
    Now, they, too, are leaving.

To pray with the saints on this lucky day
    And find the untethered whispers of an ancient dark
    In the space where Grace should be…
    It's the dread of *no more* that distresses the mind
    And encourages Heart to reach for the flame
    That it should have never lost…

…but it is the last trace of smoke in the air
    That pushes sorrow into innocent veins
    And condemns the affectionate shade to haunt
    The land of the Untouchable.

An ache that spreads,

Not the promised bite of a hope in peril,
But a shock that pillages every beloved secret
And consumes memory until
A soul would promise anything to feel the pain
That was slaughtered by the pervasive numbness
Of absent mortality.

There's no life behind these words,
    And the clovers have gone,
    Left forever,
    Abandoned,
    And not even the kiss of this lucky day,
    Nor the will of every devoted saint,
    Could save the clovers from the gardens of purgatory.

AFFECTION'S GUARD

Exquisite sorrows found in the ruins of Betrayal,
    The favoured weapons of the Lovely and Alone,
    Sit in solitude,
    Withering roses waiting for the attack they expect to know,
    An inherited chance to reject those who might come to beg and atone.

These withered roses that stretch towards the sun
    In the aching of every day,
    Only find peace when darkness comes,
    At night, when silver splinters are slyly spun;
    The rosy Betrayed plants desperation beside the roots and ruins
    Of unsummoned Justice,
    To be abandoned, to wither, to rest, to be undone.

LOVE'S LEAST FAVOURITE INHERITANCE

Heartbreak reinvents itself with every lover that it takes;
   It begins affairs to savour the essence
   Of what's lost at the end,
   And its most satiated self metamorphosizes
   Through the brave and the willing.

It does not simply favour the weak,
   Nor does it only tempt the strong…
   Heartbreak takes whomever it can,
   It feeds on the hope of every lover,
   And rejoices in the chaos it sows
   In the hearts of those who have nothing left in them
   To save what was left to them.

Heartbreak has never belonged to Love alone.
   It belongs to *us*,
   And in its presence,
   It is we,
   The bravest and the most willing,
   Who are left undone and alone.

A HEIGHT TOO FAR FOR ME

A broken heart has not enough strength to break me,
   The pieces of what *once was* will break again
   When held against all that I am now.

I *fear* what heals,
   I *shudder* when met with the heart made whole,
   The heart that beats, and bleeds, and lives
   With the shards of a memory that left trauma-clawed marks
   On the enduring soul.

Who am I to stand against every beat of hope renewed?

The numbness braces the broken against another fall,
   But Hope flies in every sky,
   And it's the adversity of ambiguity,
   Abandonment in flight,
   That imparts to me the fear that I may crash
   Or never land at all.

DEPRIVATION IS A DREAMER

The heart hides within the stories of youth
   Until reality builds a fairy tale in which it can truly exist...

A glove holds the shape of the hand
   That longs to be held,
   But it holds no warmth,
   For it is not flesh and bone,
   But an imitation held in place
   Of the missing hand.

The body in search of heat
   Finds forgery in the blanket that imitates true warmth;
   It holds no sympathy,
   Only the sensational illusion of two arms
   Wrapped around a shivering frame.
   It offers no embrace,
   There is no body.

Fairy tales are built on the hope of every youthful heart
   That longs to bring the dreams in which they live
   Into a reality they can touch...
   Into a life they can love.

THE INDULGENCE OF A MOMENT TAKEN FOR GRANTED

Am I so starved of such simple pleasure
   That I am left to find gratification,
   An ounce of Essence,
   In the mundane intimacies of ordinary lovers?

Memories, the softness of a fallen feather,
   Of moments taken *perfectly* for granted,
   The unhurried time to say,
   I love you,
   Once more,
   Is a comfort that leaves me hopefully enchanted;
   The great rise of Intimacy's grace,
   (A privilege of intimate friendship
   And deep love),
   Is Heaven's true and most beloved face.

LOVE'S JESTER

Fate's command of unearthly dreams!

It is the weary hopeful that rejects their belief
   In that which they most crave;
   When they cannot see the fruits
   Of their laborious faith,
   They enslave themselves to Mockery,
   To jest in their lack,
   Pretending not to harbour,
   Nor to seek,
   The very strength that makes them weak
   In knees so bruised,
   A soul so tired.

The hopeful cynic condemns Affection
   Under their abandoned faith's tyrannical rule,
   Makes tenderness cheap, turns it vulgar,
   But in every breath that gives life to this broken sense,
   They carry the knowing that they have always been
   Love's most devoted fool.

THE WISH YOU CRY

It's in your most desperate
   I love you
   That the soul reveals itself;
   Your sincerity is selfish,
   Your very love is greedy in its spoken form.
   This *prayer* that is ripped from your being
   Lands on unholy ground,
   But you let it go,
   You send it away…

For every word from your bruised lips
   Is a well-dressed cry
   For all the things that you've ever wanted
   But never had.

It is not your love that you give,
   But your misery,
   For it is another's love that you want,
   Another's affection that you *crave,*
   But that is a truth you will not bear,
   So it is a love you will never see.

AN IMPOSTER CREEPING UPON THE LIGHT OF DAY

Force was the name by which she called her love.

Uncontrollable,
   (Though control was not desired
   For this wild thing that kept her sane),
   It was soft, warm, and entirely hers.
   Innocence held her…until it could no more,
   For control was granted to a mimic of Love's impression,
   And so she fell beneath the Merciless and Cruel,
   One who was born to hide, smother, and tame;
   In a stranger's wild obsession,
   Her force became twisted and strange,
   And her love, as force, became the stranger
   That she had met as forceful affection.

She fought for her love,
   The goodness she bore to a gentle world,
   The grace she felt as warmth on tender skin,
   But Love fought her to an agony without end,
   A fight destined to renew in malice,
   To always and forever begin.

In the embrace she returned to a suffocating cage,
   She met twin hands,
   Alike in vision,
   (Certainly, they belonged to one and the same),
   In presence, however, they rested separate and opposed,
   Passion and Possession was the recognition
   Gifted to them by Name.
   She embraced in affection,
   But, by control, she had been trapped and hopelessly enclosed.

Through this madness of a romance so tainted and lecherous,
   She looked at what she saw
   And felt not the force of Love she had once known,
   Pure and alive,
   But the mockery of Love's beautiful design,
   (This we knew, but it was a truth she had now come to own):
   Not a force as being,
   But a force as numbed feeling.

She found herself rising in this place of understanding,
   Returning to a state of being safe and sane,
   Rising above her forced irreverence.

She dropped the twin hands that had grown cold
   In her ascent,
   And outside the reach of one who was twisted and strange,
   She found Strength,
   (Its warm hands were there to cherish and to hold),
   And with Strength, she walked.
   In hope, she went.

Caution was with her in the wake of a past
  That she now knew as her promised and peaceful path,
  And one day,
  (She could never remember what day it was,
  Simply that it had happened suddenly one day),
  She was joined by a friend she had once known well,
  A friend who was warm, and gentle, and entirely uncontrollable,
  (In truth, that was her favourite kind to think of),
  And she remembered the name of this faithful friend…
  It came to her slowly, but she did remember in the end that
  Force was the name by which she called her love.

WHEN A FLAME MET THE WIND

In the quiet night, with its gentle hue
   Of sweet memory and forgotten affection,
   I sat with a friend,
   (*Darkness was his favourite name*),
   And fell into his arms,
   Reclaiming, for a time, the love that was ours,
   Exquisite imperfection.

It was in this love that we existed,
   A soft word, a gentle caress,
   Harshness in expression, never in being,
   Though it was harshness, nonetheless!
   We performed as well as we could,
   Gave breath to our very best,
   But we were doomed at the beginning;
   This was a tragedy of the poets' design,
   Our suffering was written,
   The most beautiful, the dearest.

To fade into sweet grief was our most hopeful end.
   I wish that I could have held us
   For a time, once more,

In our hearts too shy and best intentions
Destined to bend.

It was a tender existence,
   Our love turned art,
   But now I read Tragedy in the arms of another,
   (*Darkness was his favourite name*),
   And all that had been is remembered now in the flesh
   And in the hushed whispers hiding in my heart.

THE NOTES THAT CARRY

We shared a song,
   (It was mine before it became yours,
   And still,
   In your memory,
   It belongs *faithfully* to me),
   And this is how I came to be
   A companion to Immortality.

Absence shelters us,
   Keeps us away from one another,
   (Ours was an intimacy of the most innocent kind-
   A friendship flavoured with just a drop
   Of curiosity and the light taste of romantic wine),
   For we, together, were not the ones meant to last,
   But this song and my voice in your head.

I am bound to Remembrance,
   When it awakens *that* memory of our shared moment,
   A small symphony of our shared past.

Every few years,
   (Pray it is not more),

A RAVEN IN THE SNOW

This song will float to you,
And your thoughts will drift to me,
And so I smile now at this dream with my good companion,
Immortality.

AT YOUR FEET

I hold gardenias for you…

A perfect bouquet,
   Quiet and unassuming;
   An offering to you,
   Fresh and alive,
   A gift to the one who cannot stay.

They have bloomed
   Beneath the tender care of my careful affection,
   And they will bloom again
   When the petals in these hands of mine
   Wilt and wither;
   The bouquet will remain,
   For these gardenias are for you,
   They were planted in your name.

I have more to give,
   Should desire find you in need of my gardenias,
   (A field of them grows just beyond all that you have seen
   And all that I have begun to say).
   So, *please*, find me again,

And I will give and give,
If you drop a flower along the way.

Your hands are free to pick other flowers,
   Of softer petals and sweeter scents,
   If you decide never to hold
   My bouquet again,
   But there will always be a garden of them waiting here for you,
   Still blooming, just as alive as they were before,
   Should you find yourself longing for gardenias once more.

TWO OF CUPS

Is there a phantom in your dream
   Wearing the humanity that claims my fame?

Do I haunt on in place of Presence?

Are the lingering lovers in your mind
   Making love to you with the memories
   Of me that remain?

Reverie bleeds through my veins
   With the thought that I am survived by
   The Missing,
   That you shelter an ache that echoes every word
   I might say.

To you,
   Of me,
   There is a married will fastening our likeness to a shared name,
   But the blood spilled in Fortune's favour
   Is the same poison that taints and blames
   The history of our love that,
   Once, we knew.

A RAVEN IN THE SNOW

There is a small light balanced on Whim
    That tethers us well on the hope of one,
    Breathing, always, for the promise of two.

AN AUTUMN WIND'S DREAMING

A caress of Autumn's colour:
   A breeze that finds liberty
   In the moment of Morning's first wake
   And at Evening's last splendour;
   I indulge in this bliss,
   Pretending that Autumn's breath
   Finds a beginning in your chest,
   As you admire me,
   Lovely,
   While I drift between sleep
   And your sweetness.

THE HAUNTING THAT HOLDS ME

The blankets of absent Warmth
   Have been the greatest dream,
   And the most troubling proof,
   Of a touch that I have not known
   Yet crave with a well-worn knowing…

It is the flames of Affection
   That kindle my longing,
   Though Reverie claims its name,
   And it will be in the gaze of tender love
   That I understand how inadequate Dream has been acclaimed,
   When I find that the breath of its reality
   Holds a sweetness that spirit alone cannot summon.

In this relieved reflection,
   I would dream again,
   Find warmth in an embrace that was not there,
   If it meant that I could, one day, wake
   To the reality of an awaited love and
   A warmth that we would, together, share.

A FLOWER GROWS FROM A BROKEN STONE

My hopeless devotion speaks to you,
   A siren's call to Ice and Stone;
   It is not my love that warms your heart,
   But the unwavering softness of my choice in you
   That cradles the brittleness of your being,
   Making tender your callous bones.

Under the care of a delight called Violence,
   You bled your love,
   (It was the lingering taste of copper on a mouth
   So just and fair
   That taught you loyalty,
   Dedication in a dispirited sense),
   But now you bleed your love no more,
   (Violence ran; it did not delight in me),
   For I kiss those once-stained lips,
   They are mine to cherish,
   Mine to adore…
   The taste of your vulnerability
   Belongs to me.

When the echoes of my name
   Exist, alone, on the winds
   That carry what remained of the breath
   Left inside of your chest,
   It will be remembered,
   (By whom, it is not for us to say),
   That a soul was saved in the love that came,
   (You were my hero, even if Memory leaves your name unpossessed),
   And *somewhere*,
   Ice and Stone will cradle our mended bones together,
   Because Violence came, ravished, and stained,
   But Love was a delight it could not tame,
   So Violence left;
   It could not stay.

THE BROKEN PIECES FIT

Let Vulnerability guide you
   To me,
   And we will love,
   Together,
   Like our souls have never known what exists
   After Anguish's cold bite
   Nor our hearts the emptiness of Loss's
   Last sight.
   We will carve ivory with our sweet nothings
   And create treasures, *beloved*, that will be beautiful
   Long after we have given up the mortal mirror,
   And in this, we will be endlessly remembered
   But always unfound.
   We will exist in this love,
   Alone together,
   Perish embraced and entranced,
   And find contented recognition in knowing that our love was
   Alive.

THE VOW THAT GUIDES US HOME

The scent of your soul
   Lingers on
   To find rest with me;
   Let Memory drift beyond thought of us,
   Beyond the ungrounded grief that our story
   Was written upon,
   Let us lose the night
   To again find faith in a forgotten dream.

(I have loved you in the Waking,
   In the every moment of gifted life and happy death,
   With a breast of breath,
   With lungs deprived,
   I have loved you throughout chance,
   When we found and lost time).

My call summons you on the colours of the wind,
   (It was not the earth, but the power of a breaking wave,
   That lent its colour to your eye);
   And when sweetness settles on my tongue,
   It is the innocence of your smile,
   The strength of your mind,

That tells me of your greatness,
A distance away, but always by my side.

I have not lost you,
   Nor is our story done.
   We wait, we heal, we find ourselves
   To find each other again.
   (Destiny is but a great hour that makes us one).

I hold myself to hold a little part of you,
   (And I have heard that there is a tenderness to your touch that belongs to me),
   Until the final will in that great hour has found us,
   When there is rest, and the final story is ours.

THE POETRY OF THE DARK'S DEPTH

It is the sky of darkness bound
   That holds the softness of my ever-dreaming
   Light.

The stars hide for fear of Life,
   The longing of dreamers and lonely lovers
   Holding fast to what can never be held…
   But this sky of the dark alight
   Longs for a lover so that it may never, again,
   Dream alone,
   For it's been loyal to expectant Night,
   Loved for what it can show of another's flame
   (The stars aplenty,
   A moon perfect, blessed, and bright).

The darling of a devouring grace,
   I am held as the greatest star,
   The wonder of what can always *be*
   Held within my reaching hand,
   And with the promise of my dark embrace,
   It is I who bends the sky,
   Willing darkness to my name,

To be fated and found in Sanctuary,
Softly,
And to be the ever-dreaming light
Of darkness bound.

THE MISTRESS

A love affair with life:

To seduce my days and find passion in my nights.
   Oh! I want my hours to be the whispered secrets
   From lips dripping honey,
   And I want my weeks to be the sensual smoke
   From a cigarette shared between lovers
   After Passion's favourite dance.

It is the thought of living,
   Of submitting to the colours of life
   And birthing Art itself,
   By which I am most romanced.

I will flirt with Wakefulness,
   And dance with Breath,
   And fall madly in love with the existence of it all.

A WRINKLE IN TIME

To the Bradys

Our beauty began with a *once upon a time*;
   The stories of our bodies,
   The treasured edges that grew in youth
   And blossomed in age,
   Belong to us, and us alone.
   We do not fall under the scrutiny of Time,
   For the canvas of our skin is ours to decorate,
   Ours to love.

To dance, to flirt, to fall in adoration with the reflection
   We see in the looking glass of our lives;
   To welcome change and find power in the choice
   Of defining beauty exactly as we understand it.

The beauty of Youth holds gentle hands with the elegance of Age.

We exist in the intimacy of knowing ourselves,
   So well and so completely,
   And find truth in recognizing the art
   Of our time-touched figures.

To become. To create.
   To love in age.
   To be beautiful.
   Always.

The essence of our beauty
   Tasted only as the finest vintage;
   The hands that hold the sandglass
   Of our own time are kissed with nothing
   But reverence.

In our power of exquisite acceptance,
   Of unfiltered confidence,
   May any doubt of our beauty,
   Of our love,
   Of our light,
   Exist only as a small fracture simply redefined by
   A Wrinkle in Time.

WHEN RUINS TURNED BACK INTO PALACES

My love for you,
   A plague of Affection's breed,
   Is as promised and sure
   As the binding between the Innocent
   And the inevitable tragedy that finds companionship in their misery.

To consume is my touch,
   But you bear it with arms that reach,
   Eyes that beg for more;
   I strip you, undone, to wander and seek,
   But you endure it with wonder,
   You see to adore;
   As I drink the spirit of your light,
   With the bleeding lips of Taint,
   You stay and gaze,
   The flower that blooms under Time's chosen midnight.

When I am the ruin promised by the chaos of the Insane,
   In the devastation wrought by the same hands that sign my name,
   It will be with the great Misplaced that you find me…
   Waiting,

Wanting,
Hoping,
For there you are, always, with the Unrelenting and Unafraid.

Forgiveness is a smile on the face
   Of the one who made me love my name,
   (The greatest of Love's many incarnations),
   A gift to cherish,
   To become under the touch of wishing Woe,
   The havoc of hopeful desperation,
   And find the audacity to believe that I am loved.

Your love for me,
   The sweet breath of Miracle's song,
   Is as promised and pure
   As the bond between the Innocent
   And the sworn tragedy that had been a fairy tale all along.

WHERE WE FALL

The imperceptible follies
   Of the descending melodies
   Written in our name…
   Shall we take a moment to fall
   Before we spend a life apart?
   To ruin ourselves on the bodies
   We can hold,
   Share a breath, and meet soul for soul
   In love?

With spinning visions in the stillness of dream,
   Perhaps flight will not find us as we fall,
   And in the finale of the broken mass of our humanity,
   We will leave what we were last given:
   Us.

THE LAST PETALS OF LOVE'S REGRET

For Glory, I have died…
   Was there honour in this end?

To have lived with every exquisite expression of life,
   To die with the taste of it all upon pale, grinning lips
     Should have been a great farewell to the soul that was gone,
     To the bone and the flesh and the pain that had been me.

But it was not the taste of life that saw me to my death,
   It was the breath of your love that last I tasted
   Upon frozen lips,
   And though Glory carried me to the end,
   I would fight the Great Shadow when he came for me
   If I could live again just for the chance
   To die for your love,
   To die for you,
   To die *with* you…

If this end was not my end,
   And Eternity gave me just a moment's breath
   To find you again,
   Then in my arms, you'd be;

For Glory, I would not die,
   Because the greatest honour that I have known
   Is the love that you have gifted,
   The love that I have always carried with me.

PHANTOM PAINS

What is Grief if not Love in disguise?

We *wear* the pain of our grief
    As a privilege.

We *bear* the honour of remembering our love;
    We feel phantom pains of its gentle touch upon our hopeful hearts
    (An embrace for our broken bodies and sorrowing spirits).

Our grief:
    A testament to a love
    Once known,
    To a love
    Once touched,
    To a love
    Never lost.

THE GHOSTS THAT VISIT THE DEAD

Weep for me when I am gone.

When I am held forever by Nature's grace,
    Rest above me,
    Bring to me the warmth that I once knew,
    (This is what I remember of an earthy embrace)
    And water the ground with your gentle melancholy.

Weep,
    And in my eternal slumber,
    I will,
    For one last time,
    Feel the mortal grief,
    (A now absent touch),
    Of your infinite love.

AFTER

If Forever takes me into its ever-changing hands,
   If I become lost in a grip that humanity cannot feel,
   Will you challenge Memory to follow me?
   Will you stretch through time,
   Broken, bested, and battle-hungry,
   To keep me alive?

Your challenge, my dear, is to breathe…

Breathe for this life that I have lost,
   Breathe for the life that you have lost in me,
   For the world has not lost the soul I was,
   Because *you* were the light that kept me alive,
   You were the very best breath between my lungs and life.

You are the very best of me.

Forever will be a friend,
   As Life holds you, my lover.
   In the days that I see you live,
   I will hold Breath again
   In the ecstasy of your wonder,

AFTER

And in the life that you have yet to lose,
Shaping body and dedicating spirit
To repentance, remembrance, and release,
At last, my dear,
In this,
I will find my promised and heavenly peace.

LOVE'S REMEMBRANCE

We have found this love in the wistful moments
   Of our delicate mortality,
   And with the passing of Day,
   Through the shelter of tender Night,
   We love,
   And because of that,
   We *live* as no other soul has lived before.
   Our bodies are doomed,
   So touch me, kiss me, love me,
   Until flesh becomes Unfeeling
   And our one mind falls into the Unknowing.
   The mystery our souls' departure
   Is a story for a different day…
   Today, we will love.
   Tomorrow, we will love.
   Together, we will love
   Until the roses grow from our buried bodies
   And fill the air with the sweet essence
   Of our *forever*.

WHAT MELODY KNEW OF US

The stage was set for our destined show,
    And it was in the darkness of our final seconds,
    Before dance transformed us into Vision,
    Where Enchantment was found.

Hypnotic spectres haunted our every step
    As a haunted audience fell into a fantasy
    Of Love's design.
    Impassioned sorrow met with the soft touch
    Of eternal pleasure,
    And there was life in every breath,
    Fate was found in every line.

The people watched,
    For Desperation held their gaze,
    And Hope showed a glory
    That it would never let fade.
    The people watched,
    And we laughed,
    Because we were alive in this show,
    And still, they watched,
    Feeling echoes of this life that they would not grasp,

This life that they could not know,
And we laughed some more.

There are still echoes of this fabled show
   (For, surely, a fable it must have been),
   And Melody softly dances now,
   Speaking of a stage and two rhythmic souls
   Who once put on the very best of what two lovers could be.

OLD SOULS TETHERED TO THE WAKING

It was not Youth I craved
   On the soft nights of helpless devotion,
   But our love and rest within Embrace.

The wickedness of juvenile follies
   Held no temptation for us,
   The two who bore Temptation
   From the womb of joined passion;
   Age held me no more than Time
   Ever could,
   For I was tethered to you
   And our joined grasp on Sensation.

It was you I craved
   On the helpless nights of our promised tenderness,
   Devoted to nothing but our
   Impatient innocence.

This was just one,
   (*One!*)
   Of the many nights of our eternal light,

(*The stories of old still carry our names*),
So wide-eyed Youth found no one when,
Clumsily, in the night,
With promise and fascination,
It came.

Our love is the Innocent,
   We find rest in its shadow,
   We find purpose in its glory,
   And in its spirit, it finds us,
   Always,
   Softly sleeping.

THE PEACE IN REST

We deserve a gentle end,
   You and I,
   After trials tire of unspoken resolutions
   Made in our name,
   And what chose to forget
   Now finds peace in the choice to forgive,
   A final gift to our fated grave.

We will spend the last of our breaths
   Giving life,
   Holding Youth within arm's reach between us,
   Remembrance holding steadfast against enclosing Night,
   (Fickle are the memories that refuse to bend),
   And Time has been generous in our keeping,
   But we deserve this final peace,
   You and I,
   When all is done,
   When we are at our end.

THE CONSTELLATION OF OUR NAME

That night, we were the stars;
   In a sky that softly held our love,
   It was the late hour's gleam
   That made us brave and hid our scars.
   Bright and sure, we burned,
   Dearly,
   In the darkness sound, held above.

Together, we knew what was found
   Beyond a midnight dreamer's wish,
   (We were the stars to which that solemn prayer
   Had been sleepily bound),
   But a passing thought of the brilliance before a dream,
   We were the bright things at midnight that were made to be missed,
   (Too far to be loved, too close to be seen).

Never once did we part, nor did we divide,
   In that splendid place of Miracle,
   Where we were the first star to be held
   In the universe of a single night
   And with the promise of a never-ending sky.

We burned to breathe, existed to explore,
   What was gifted to us on a chance so destined
   Was the pleasure of flight to love as we soared.
   A thousand moons, whispers of light,
   Remembering us, always, for the gleaming
   And how brave we were to ignite
   Our love, as stars, burning on that night.

III

THE FLIGHT OF WISDOM'S NAME

THE QUESTIONS ASKED BETWEEN CRADLE AND GRAVE

To find hope in the meaningful,
   Though what is meaning if not the End?
   To find challenge and contentment in the meaningless,
   Though what is meaningless if not the Beginning?

To live for weary Life
   So that it may reach desperate Death,
   And balanced between blackened claws and warming palms,
   Death may live,
   Neither at the end nor the beginning,
   And it will mean all that it was ever meant to be,
   And that will be all.

TRAGEDY'S HYPNOSIS

There is something within the shared soul
   Of our lost humanity
   That is inspired by the presence of Tragedy.

The devastating beauty of our immortal beloved,
   (Tragedy is a melody when spoken correctly),
   Compels and attracts in its perfect name,
   Makes poets and victims of
   The defeated, insane, unlucky, and brave.

It is a temptation born for our perfect failures,
   A siren's call on the edge of our best efforts,
   And we fall beneath a collapse we prayed would never come,
   A chaos we secretly hoped would come to be our reaper.

The greatest known secret is the one we keep together,
   The Affair of Tragedy,
   The Keeper of every name,
   And we live to wait, to see the day
   When our frightening fantasies come alive,
   And Tragedy comes to lay its claim.

TO LIVE PAST MEMORY

To outlive Legacy…

What do we become when we grow past the legacies of our greatness,
   We nameless creatures who watch as
   Humanity's inheritance bears our name?
   In a world that idolizes the spirit we have sacrificed,
   A spirit that sustains hope as we live as phantoms
   In the ruins of Possibility,
   We rot in the decay of Dynasty's tradition.

What have we become in the wake
   Of our great purpose?
   Who are we when we reach the end of our meaning
   Before we have reached the end of our lives?

Where was the fault in the hero's journey
   For me to have been left with an epilogue of peace?
   In the fires of Glory, I have fought,
   And through the great fight, I have survived,
   But can I be a hero if, for my torch, I have lived and not died?

I am the hollowed soldier:

A saviour who saved the world,
Then lived too long and saw it all die.
I should have lost myself for the triumph of Truth,
(Truth *has* prevailed,
But has chained me to its immortality);

Now I sit,
   Alone and weary,
   In the ruins of Memory,
   Trying to recall the moment I missed the path
   To what should have been my chosen end,
   And in this silence of a world shaped by my glory,
   In a world haunted by the ghosts of a time I fought to change,
   I am remembered but hopelessly sacrificed to these unending twilight days.

HEIRLOOMS

Memory does not possess me in my dreams,
   Nor in the daylight fancies decorated by treasures
   Of another time;
   What was left to me simply exists
   As the antiqued proof that it was me,
   Alone,
   Who was left to be,
   Existing not with the possessions and wealth
   Of my loved ones, in a lost time, still living,
   But walking beside the good mimic and my best friend,
   Memory.

I am the heirloom,
   Loved and left,
   To be Remembrance in my remembering,
   A ghost that haunts on in place
   Of what did not stay to possess me,
   To dust with tears this beloved space
   That was left to a living thing who no longer
   Recognizes her breathing,
   Nor the spirit in her own breath.

WHAT BECAME OF AN OPENED DOOR

Bastard keys and rusty locks,
   Holding curve and metallic taste to devoted Memory;
   Impression's gift to hands too nimble,
   Too delicate,
   To craft what can be held through time,
   (There is history in what can be forgotten,
   A purpose in all that was once left,
   A molded key, polished to shine).

THE GIFT OF TIME

Life held me to a century,
   Once,
   Then held me again, too kindly.

Immortality, with softness spun by the hand that brought it essence,
   Was much too soft a word to speak of the spirit it bore
   To every age;
   The tapestries,
   (It does not matter which ones, for they all tether under the same name),
   Were woven, in Seam, with the very colour of my spine;
   I found kinship in the measure of a year's seasons
   And through a body in its every mortal phase.

In the aging fables known by different names,
   (They are one story, shared twice too many),
   I remained, the only character to reappear,
   Reimagined and unchanged,
   Growing weary instead of growing old.

To shout is to find my own voice
   In an echo from the place set forth,

Still, I say,
"Come have me, Decay! Let me see
That beneath the human, there exists a
Beautiful vulgarity of bone!"

(I wish not to rot as a living thing,
  But to rest faithfully,
  Finally,
  In that awaited place of an earthly bed
  And a heavenly home).

I am bound within the fragments of our great history
  With the intimacy married to me by
  A far-reaching night and the dreaming of a day;

I was held to a century,
  Once,
  In a grip as unrelenting as it was kind,
  And now I have memory where there used to be mystery
  In what many a century holds,
  But what I know now lives only with me,
  And what I remember,
  I remember alone.

A SEANCE OF MY SETTLED SELF

I am the haunting that echoes through:

A possessed spirit, possessing me;
   The loved thing of forgotten graces;
   An affirmation of ghostly dread
   That astonishes the Living, tenderly.

There are phantoms here,
   In whatever space this may be,
   Who, in fancies and ghoulish follies of the dearly who never departed,
   Divine spirit from Life's poetic mystery.

Shades existing outside the colour of a mind,
   Breathing through remembrance,
   Wandering to Memory,
   Find, in their deaths,
   Lost possessions, love left, and a touch of life
   Through the haunting.

JUST A WHISPER

I am the condemned voice of the Forgotten.

Doubtful lips have held my death
   When utterance fell hush
   And lovers lost the last word
   Of their first and only love;
   I am the gleam of sweat and creeping blush
   On a sinner's face when secrets of their sin
   Find their refuge of Atonement out of reach
   And up above;
   A widow's lament at dusk
   Is a favourite of mine,
   When languishing shadows dance and echo grief
   Across still and silent stone.

I am everywhere you cannot find me.

What was left, abandoned, held, and unheard
   Will strike each quiet mind to chaos,
   And I,
   The condemned ghost of the Forgotten,
   Will find my voice again when the defeated plead,

Mercy waits,
And I have the last and final word.

THE SANDGLASS WHISPERS

May Father Time make a daughter of me,
   To hold me gently,
   To see me off into a finite oblivion,
   An endlessness with an end,
   A quiet dark with a delicate morning light.

Let sandy fingers drop visions and splendour
   Upon the restless children of absent Dream;
   To hold in softness, to suspend,
   The conscious above the waking world,
   Holding innocence away from the Shadowed and Unseen.

Thoughts become me in my slumber,
   But unsettled Night takes this body for shelter,
   And I am awake.

Sleep is not mine.
   I am but an orphaned dreamer,
   Looking for the tender care of the Settled and Sane,
   To hear melodies in a softly sung nursery rhyme,
   To perhaps dream again in the warm arms
   Of my wayward father, unreachable Time.

THE NAKEDNESS OF YOUR FAVOURITE THOUGHT

Do not ask absent dreams
   To become the great stories
   Of your gentle curiosities;
   Let them fall beneath the rested Wicked,
   To die with the taste of hope on lips painted and bare,
   Burn those old stories,
   The ones that say,

"Ah! You see it, don't you?
   The undressing of my desires,
   Roses soft, petals fair".

Burn those old stories!

In a great gentleness,
   Rewrite what is born from the dearly Inspired,
   Dream in absence,
   And find a myth to match in curiosity
   The courage you have to love
   What you most admire.

THE GENTLEST OF NIGHTTIME FANCIES

Oh, Gentle Night!

Give me sleep upon a bed of petals,
   A bouquet gifted by lavender hands
   And softly laid by my most beloved fantasies.
   Embrace me with silk woven by satisfied stars,
   And let the peace of this slumber
   Be the greatest of a star's living legacy.

Keep from me the thorns of Terror,
   Let them worship every sigh that leaves my lips
   While I am held askance,
   Breathing the fragrance of Reverie in
   A content and untroubled sleep.

Oh, Gentle Night!

Let me land,
   Not fall,
   In the garden of enchanted dreams and fated chance!
   Sing to me the lullabies of old

So that I may delight in this world
Of strange visions and friendly strangers,
(Where all and none are as they seem).

Let Rest awaken my slumbering eyes
   So that I may rise and see,
   (The morning is too bright,
   Too loud, for a dreamer like me),
   And I will cry out again
   For the sleep that I knew….
   My sweet, gentle, and ever-loving Night.

A PAST LIFE LAID TO REST

Forsaken to a breathing where there was no breath,
   I found not enough water to drown me.
   With a heaving chest,
   Dying,
   Pain left me at the feet
   Of the three children of Mortality:

Ache was there in the lungs
   That sought something light,
   The spirit flowered in breath,
   In air;
   Relief was loud upon my ear
   To drown, not me,
   But the crash of waves,
   A harsh wetness upon my fear;
   Warmth dried skin too wet to hold,
   And I felt the weight of it,
   Not sea but sun,
   In place of where I thought should be
   The cold.

So was borne these graces to the carved marble

Of my feet,
And they, the beautiful children of Mortality,
Saved a drowning thing,
And I loved in them what I could not drown beneath.

THE CONSTELLATIONS OF MY SKIN

The stars are devotion,
   Pure light and fervent faith,
   And I, the celestial muse,
   A canvas for their creation.

This body held in their reverence,
   (For they fell to shine
   As vibrant veins and bright,
   Ever-searching eyes),
   Is an abused and beloved delight;
   It is easy to condemn mirrored visions
   While holding to the ignorance
   That the light worn
   Is the same light beheld,
   In love,
   On a clear and unclouded night.

I am at the mercy of unrepentant Wonder,
   Which stands with me beneath the stars,
   (In these hands, I hold myself).
   So the sky is held in my gaze,
   And in my good embrace,

And it is here I learn Midnight's favourite secret:
That one cannot love the stars
Without loving their time-honoured creations,
Us, the celestial others.

THE SILK OF SALVATION

In the sinful act's great grief
   Of speckled memory and sweating peace,
   I found the grace of promise,
   Of hope.

With grievance done,
   And the relief of unsullied folly
   Walking me home,
   I found rest in Gratitude.

It was the blessing of a fall
   That let me rise,
   To hold my spirit up to Dignity
   And unveil the great design
   Of being alive.

A CALLING BLESSED

The world may not choose me
   To wear its destruction or to bear its tragedy,
   But I will stand,
   Still,
   For someone's redemption,
   (That great gift of a forgiving thing known to us),
   And the world will be reborn on a thought,
   Belonging in a whisper of humanity.

To be forgotten would be a bitter peace,
   But the sweetness of a remembered misfortune,
   The life and death of a martyred truth,
   Promises a memory so pure
   That the shadows of inevitable Death himself
   Cannot touch it.

LEGEND'S FIRST AND LAST LAUGH

The beginning of the end,
   (A spark that lit the torches of Finale),
   Began when I walked into a moment
   That revealed itself to be the rest of my life.

Unbeknownst to Soul,
   Or to the mediocrity of the everyday,
   Weighted steps carried me to Destiny,
   And where they began,
   I could not say,
   For perhaps they never did begin;
   Perhaps the weight had rested,
   Silent and simmering,
   Always,
   Until the relief of a first breath's wail
   First echoed in the world.

With triumphant trepidation,
   I flew as I fell,
   Touching the waters of Becoming
   While laughing in the sky of the Unforgotten.

I had met my end before my promised start,
    And there was peace in the Forgiving
    That held me to the ground
    As my spirit reached for a limit that had yet to be known,
    A limit that had yet to begin.

A TESTAMENT TO SOUL

The grace of this humanity finds an understanding,
   A pardon to its follies,
   Through the art of Being,
   (The creations born from our creation).

This is how I explain my *humanness*-
   Through words,
   Through touch,
   Through breath…

There can be no direct thought
   To explain the very nature of what we are,
   Save for the mosaic built through the ages
   Of what was left by us,
   Alone,
   And through what was presented by us,
   Together,
   When we came to be underneath
   A sky so open, within the burning of one great star.

SIN'S ALLURE

This delight of the Mischievous and Untamed
   Beckons Temptation with a whisper;
   Barely a breath,
   And in Mayhem's memories,
   Perfection falls to ecstasy (silk, seduction, and faintly played symphonies).

To float in waters dark and tainted,
   Soothed, loved, and desperately intoxicated
   By this sea of black-satin sin!
   The flirtation of two wills balanced between eager breath,
   Warmth from the kindling of a well-tended hearth,
   I am found where I have come to rest:
   In a body that feels,
   In a mind that wanders,
   In a heart that beats within my life-caging breast.

This is my mystery,
   It has found delight in my company,
   And I weave with the strings of Enchantment and Ease,
   For it was my summons under beguiling Night,
   Alone,

That called this beastly beloved to me.

APPETITE

An insatiable appetite for life!

I crave Experience and sit hungry with Memory.
   I am unsatisfied with half-prepared moments.
   I need substance!

Feed me life, and I will live forever.

THE EDGE

Standing against the world,
   We are here,
   Carrying the weight of a humanity we have known,
   Conscience threadbare,
   (We are cloaked in Being made of that very thread),
   The Earth brings us forth again,
   Stretching tall, brittle limbs to see us through
   With desperate care;

The winds offer promise for a world so tender,
   But Liberation is felt in the marrow of every soul's beloved bones.
   We are the Promised offered on the winds
   To mend what is seen in the cracks of the broken,
   To be the faithful light,
   Unshaken,
   The prophesized promise to always win.

THE PURITY OF LOVE-DRIVEN NECROMANCY

Destruction will find me smiling,
   When dust alone cradles the memory of buried, beloved bones,
   For I knew him, and we loved beyond
   The aging of bodies longing to find earth,
   Whispers of the world begging to go home,
   (Our love bore Time to Life,
   When breath was just a thought,
   When Thought had not yet become).

When that grave hour has gone an hour past,
   There I will be,
   Smiling,
   And echoes of our love will rise in place
   Of shouting Terror who made brave men stumble
   Where they stood.
   What swallowed the light of half-told histories
   Will know what that hour offers to the Grave
   When forces greater than fragile Corruption
   Find voice in the quiet before awakening.

The beating of our one heart,

Scorching and saving the emptied veins of soil turned to ash,
Will resurrect the immortal spirits of every mortal love
That held breath and graced flesh,
And this spirit of long-buried light will Become
In ruin.

The world will be loved back into being
   With the tender touch of Redamancy,
   And when Sight comes again in the warmth of our remembered rising,
   Creation will find me, at last, smiling.

RISING WITH A HERO'S NAME

There was a promise to save the world,
   A destined task for the chosen among us;
   Labouring Destiny bore Heroism
   Between the seconds of forsworn redemption
   And prophesized peace,
   And on the peaks of everything that we have ever known,
   Heroes came to be.

They grew into their individual fates
   And emerged through the crafty hands of Fate itself.
   They fought for their reason
   While being fought at every step by those with whom,
   In destined allyship,
   They were always meant to share this reason.

In the ashes of Hope was where the biggest battle began,
   And in this greyness,
   Almost-heroes continue to sit,
   Shouldering the burden of their humanity
   With willing discontent.
   The price of ignorance,
   The consequence of living this malignancy

In opposition to united endeavour,
Is bitter disquiet and chosen inability,
A disappointment to once-labouring Destiny.

These are the Unrealized,
   Pawns for the enemy,
   Another task for the Chosen;
   A reason renewed,
   A glimpse of an ash-ridden world,
   And the threat of a world rid of hope.

These Unrealized sit as they are,
   Sit as they wish to be,
   And this glimpse is the greatest
   Weapon for the endeavouring Chosen,
   A reminder to change what they see,
   Not to lose themselves in believing they are meant to save
   What does not want to be saved.
   Heroes can change what is seen in the world,
   But it is Love,
   And Love alone,
   That saves everything that exists
   And all that is meant to be.

Destiny bore the spark of these heroes
   At the feet of Desolation
   And into the hands of Awakening
   Knowing that the greatest power would be
   The grief that could not crush
   What was left of the ones last standing.

UNWRITTEN SANCTUARIES

The stars have been my favourite keeper
   For every secret I was too scared to hold.
   It has never been the darkness that gave me a sanctuary
   Of a burden laid to rest,
   But the forgiving light of sheltered memory
   That bore the heaviness of a soul growing old.
   What was written in the patterns of Slumber's sky
   Was a moment once felt,
   An entire life lived to its very best.
   What exists beneath an infinity that never changes
   Are the people who do not know when to stop.
   Through every wink of a star being born,
   And from the Phoenix seen on ordinary nights
   When people sleep, and a star dies,
   The Soul of many is remembered,
   Held safe by the sanctuary of stars,
   The Great Keeper within the night sky.

FIREWORKS

We live, as humanity, in the reflection of fireworks.
    Or, perhaps, they perform as a reflection of us:
    A pantomime of Life's design.

Perhaps,
    We exist *together*
    In an understanding,
    Not consciously accepted but intrinsically felt,
    That our beauty,
    That our light,
    Exists for its impermanence.

With the hope and wonder of a temporary thrill,
    Against the backdrop of a celebratory night,
    Fireworks are sent into the sky
    With a burst of colour and an expression of light.

The sound rings out,
    Confidently,
    Proudly,
    And is well remembered through the echoes
    That continue to ring in the minds

Of those who were present for the show,
And is wondered at,
And slightly missed,
By those who were too far away.

For a short time,
    The sparks fight the stars for space in the darkened sky,
    And win,
    For but a moment,
    With their shocking brilliance and uniting joy.

You and I,
    The fireworks lit by ambitious hands,
    Enjoy this space,
    On this night,
    To fill the sky
    And express our light.

We exist,
    So loudly,
    So brightly,
    So beautifully,
    To then exist no more.

ONE MOMENT LIVING IN TIME TWICE

A farewell minute with Second Chance,
   (What flies beyond the day you lived
   Are the phantoms that find you
   At an unhappy death).

What is sought, and what must one evade,
   In the spent second relived
   Amongst an hour loved and left?

Such is the chance of dreams never given,
   A gift not meant to find hands,
   Just a whisper, *not alive*,
   (It knew life once, but it met with
   Another Will's demands,
   And what never was could not survive,
   Beyond a minute of a second chance's
   First and last time).

ANTIQUE BOOKS

An enchantment begins and a tale ends
   Along the spines of books
   That sit as artifacts,
   Carefully placed and softly touched,
   Upon the shelves that they have crossed rivers of time to call
Home.

Some are weathered with age,
   Others are blessed by it,
   But they all hold Age's favourite gift:
   Memory.

Some memories hide deep within the caverns of folded pages,
   Others are obvious in their existence,
   With the curves of someone's angelic print
   Dancing between the lines of Story…
   Some memories remain unknown to me still,
   Though beheld by eager eyes,
   They remain unrecognized by Inquisition,
   For some treasures belong to the books alone.

History has carried them to me,

And so I carry them along,
Familiarizing them with my days and nights,
Finding a thrill in knowing that I now belong
To their immortality.

Souls, long departed, reach over my shoulder
    To point to a favoured line or a perfect ring on yellowed paper
    Left by spilled coffee and their favourite mug.
    I carry these books and find the weight
    Of all the lives that they have touched,
    And I wonder at the lightness that has yet to be filled
    By all the lives that will come after
    My time with them is done.

I hold them tenderly,
    Gently,
    And in the stillness of a moment,
    I am holding hands with someone I will never meet.

MY DEVOTION

Tragedy bleeds,
   (I found Prophecy in the patient grief
   Of an agony that made my favourite wounds weep);
   It is faithful,
   The pain that etches religion onto the softness
   Of open-minded Memory.

Heartache breaks in the same hour that love repossesses,
   And it is effervescent Hope on the edge of every moment
   That sees to heal,
   To bless,
   What is left of the divinity in mortal veins and damning breath;
   This peace is what I am,
   An ever-willing tragedy and always-lovely fortune
   Living in Life until I find rest in ever-waiting, loving Death.

A CELESTIAL PERSPECTIVE

On a night of a thousand wonders,
   I graced the stars,
   (Delight carried me from that night's expected slumber),
   And amongst the vast and inky sky,
   I looked upon the Despised and Devoted of a great world living,
   So near and desperately far.

It was Life that held my gaze;
   So familiar,
   This face that looked at me,
   Yet shy and strange!
   Up above, did some part of me remain down below?
   I could not see one thing at all,
   Except for the great One of all,
   With no one heart left alone in its triumphant beating.
   There was neither peace nor chaos in this vivid dream,
   (For this must have been a vision of Dream's design),
   Only light, constant and gleaming.

In this celestial dignity of perfect balance,
   I observed with the stars,
   Saw the essence of goodwill and yearning,

Loved with them in meaning,
And it was there that I learned,
On this night of a thousand wonders,
That stars,
Astonishing and ever-present,
Gaze upon us to remind them that there is beauty in the burning.

VERITAS

To touch Truth in pursuit of a petal,
   That softly fallen thought that dances on the walls
   Of a room held darkly and blessed by flame,
   The lips of some bright thing tasting the breath of some long-buried dread,
   A kiss of the earth sheltered between cradle and grave;
   To let a dream just be a dream,
   Choosing the moon, its dashing white,
   To see me through as a phantom of hidden dreaming,
   The treasured and unjustly fabled bride of Night;
   To understand the Remembering,
   That some are born to marry their memory to Solace
   Or to be summoned in the fractures of a reverie;
   To know that there is terror in loving and being loved,
   Dearly,
   And that death is not Death until the day it comes for me.

A MIDNIGHT VISITOR

Death saw me,
   Kindly,
   And waited faithfully at my door.

(The scent of a floral Dark
   Grew stronger through the fragrant seasons
   Of an abundant life;
   It was this grim essence of a waiting reaper
   That I, in age, found myself longing for).

Life was given the promise
   Of holding me up to Light,
   When shadows took Grace
   From my aging lines,
   When a mortal mark was left
   On the Undying of this world;
   A final breath,
   An echo of being,
   Evidence of a body that had been dispossessed,
   Life held me,
   Until it could hold me no more.

Death,
   My faithful friend, and Fear's favourite adversary,
   The awaited visitor behind my
   Still and silent door,
   Was a silhouette of innocent immortality
   Cloaked in the vibrance of a great morality.

We held hands
   And left what I had been chosen to leave behind,
   (We did not walk through *that* door),
   And in this intimacy of the In-Between,
   Death walked me,
   Faithfully,
   Through the gates of awaited Sanctuary.

A FAREWELL

Innocence holds what the Dark consumes
   In greater age,
   (A meeting between Essence
   And the end of bloom).
   There is a taste to mortality that savours the life
   That surrenders to its claim…
   This is the breathing,
   (The peace and its pain).

What is lived beyond the day
   That a babe was born
   Is what is known
   As what is left as a last love note
   At the final goodbye;
   A crystalline spirit in withering form,
   We are lucky to live and forever blessed to die.

Held *gently* in the space
   Of the deep, long breath between
   The embrace to which we are born
   And the Great Welcome in which we are buried,
   There will be a farewell,

(A step away, a return to those
Who once shared our blood),
And the most simple and ever-enchanting
Part of it all
Will be that we loved.

AUTUMN'S WELCOME

Miracle's chance on broken whim,
    It is the essence of light to shine through break,
    For the bird to fly after Nature's healed its broken wing.

Let it be merry,
    The night's disguise of starlit tapestries,
    Its silken strands woven by a late hour's paradise,
    The sound of bells on air that's still,
    Breath to breathe,
    An honest traveller's goodwill
    Through the light of an everlasting evening…

To say farewell to Nature's green,
    A greeting of charm, magic, and delight,
    To bid the good spirits welcome,
    And to all else,
    A good and spirited night.

THE BREATHING PERHAPS

To take on Chance with a tempest's breath,
   And believe that the spirits of the haunting light
   Are our souls carried back to us,
   From another place,
   (The suspended belief of an awaited time),
   Holding to our chests
   The best of blinding Night,
   As we stand,
   As we have stood,
   Together in every life.

Perhaps is a bond that weaves and binds
   The threads of our souls
   To what another *perhaps* in the Great Lost
   Left behind;
   We know what was left
   As we stand as what came to be
   From a century's air,
   (We were carried away at abundant dusk
   To find at dawn the century left bare).

To know a soul without learning a name,

THE BREATHING PERHAPS

We were observed by haunted spectres
That lived before our feet could carry the weight
Of so great a game.
Chest to chest with centuries for breadth,
This breath is union,
Between a petaled past and a flowering future,
Not apart, but endlessly and forever the same.

WHAT WHISPERS ON A MEADOW GREEN

Faintly,
   Power speaks; awakened by a spark,
   Carried by breath,
   Resting in the flesh,
   The eloquence of its speech is found in everything
   Untouched by Word,
   Though Word charades as its greatest glory.

Killed by a spark,
   Smothered by breath,
   Rotting in the flesh,
   There is Power, faintly speaking.
   It is unheard.
   It is unspoken.
   It is unclaimed.

To be awakened to your spark,
   To bless with your breath,
   To settle into your flesh,
   Power is, faintly,
   Until it speaks through you.

Sanity is tethered so that you remain free,
   For Valour holds darkness,
   Despair clutches the light,
   And, in gripping fists, you wield both
   So that you may stand, and live, and revel in Mastery's immortality;
   Believe, perhaps, for a time,
   In your chosen dream,
   And pray that you have chosen the noble side of memory,
   Because Power is still power,
   Even when spoken faintly.

A REMEMBRANCE WAITING

Something new to challenge the old,
    The twisted visions of Destiny's deed
    That bring me the Silent's wish to end
    The anguish of self-born slavery;
    The world works on this rhythm of hope,
    When Innocence, Faith, and Nature meet together
    (It is the flight of folly that makes Youth bold).

The golden world still exists,
    Just beyond what we once lost in the willows,
    It echoes,
    It rattles with its ancient plea:

Remember me in the After,
    When that foretold time comes to be...

THE KEY IS FOUND IN HISTORY

On the winds of the Deathless,
   The scent of kings, who sat alone on velvet thrones,
   Is carried to me, and I come to know solemn Victory and unforgiven Sin.
   I follow this path of Humanity's great inheritance,
   In the ruins left by Time's unremembered Kin,
   And by the persistent light of a pale and ancient moon,
   I trace the footsteps of ambitious Affection and earned Contentment
   Given to me by the heavy steps left by a secret swain
   On another time's ordinary afternoon.

I look for the maidens and mothers
   In the grace of wildflowers planted in hope
   At the end of some violent tyrant's bloody reign,
   And I can almost see, in the rays of a blazing sun
   That set long ago,
   The children who sat on wagons headed home,
   Those who grew into memories that only History,
   Alone, could say it knew.
   Uncovered, once entwined by the growing green
   Of a budding vine,
   Is the last kiss of someone's first love,

Painted through the lingering romance
In the still and silent air.

What was found and lost has now been claimed,
    For the mark of legendary kings is ours to bear,
    And the stories of peasants past carry our names.
    It is here, in rivers of history flowing through bodies
    That wear the faces of those loved before our time,
    Where we find Truth…

We are the Descendants, the ruins of a forgotten age!
    We bear witness to the resurrection of Thought!
    We are the Deathless, once more,
    To be, again, the bygone splendour,
    A foundation made from the Forgotten,
    To build this age, to faithfully and finally remember.

WHISPERS ON THE WIND

The threads of the shadow are but smoke
   In the tapestry of this humanity;
   What we know as Light is carried on the winds
   Of what we call Time,
   And the Great Whisper is spoken
   To the ears that listen,
   Of the ones who came before,
   The ones who have yet to be,
   And this is what remains
   To us who believe in our tricky lore,
   (In that grand place of our home,
   Where stories are lived before they are told).

The beastly creations who carry that divine spark,
   We live now until we breathe no more,
   But in the vastness of a collective breath,
   We become to be Light,
   We cross to Night as the magic dark,
   And the words we speak are echoed
   In every life;
   They are carried, still, on those tricky winds,
   Haunting, lulling, those listening insomniacs

To a gentle rest,
(It is the sound of rustling leaves on dancing trees
That knows our voices best).

In the yearning rise and great fall
    Of an empire that wore many names,
    Ashes were left to mark,
    At our feet,
    Where, *always*, we stand,
    The unmarked, nameless graves
    Of lives that spoke, that went,
    That never ceased to be.
    The nameless will rise again,
    Life for a life in that well-worn tapestry,
    To find the tended and tethered curiosities
    That, in great hope, were rendered
    In the place where history was lived before it was remembered.

There is no arresting breath
    In so many a name,
    They come to echo the ancient shouts of Time,
    To reimagine the silent softness of Age,
    And it will be known, left, and missed
    That the whisper of a forgotten dynasty
    Is the spoken legacy of a dynasty that once lived.

Epilogue

THE YOUNG LADY BELLRINGER

The young lady bellringer
   Is sleepless in her toil of resounding a remembrance
   To the facelessness of her majesty;
   She echoes, she calls on,
   Bringing Voice to the softness
   That has slithered as silence amongst the Undisturbed,
   (It was the Craven, bound,
   That held Fortune's favour,
   But she, an echoing thing,
   Is now the one who Compels,
   Bearing myth to memory through sound).

There is a plea in monotony
   That begs for ruin,
   And the young lady bellringer stands upon the Sleeping
   And holds in her chest the brazen of a song,
   Whispers it to the bell,
   And allows a single strike upon precious metal
   To be her call;
   She watches to see what Becomes in her summoning,
   What ancient dark flees and what troubled dream wakes,
   (She waits because the young lady knows

A RAVEN IN THE SNOW

That a bell, once struck, cannot be unrung).

A gladness creeping upon rotting wood,
   She, who hears echoes in the silence,
   Breaks the haunting of so still a place,
   Gives unto the shrouded lane a chance to love
   The faith that has soundly stood.

The young lady bellringer holds
   A moment to the Remembering,
   (She collects thoughts for her bell
   In place of where a rust would settle),
   She calls out, echoes on,
   Respires in a whisper,
   This once young lady,
   The first of the bellringers.

Acknowledgments

This poetry collection was lived long before it was written; the greatest dream (too ambitious for me to hold but forever blessed to be held by) is the privilege of sharing Truth through a poetic word or a romantic thought. This dream is mine to live and to honour, but without the beautiful souls who have so graciously dedicated their belief to me, this collection would have found no other reader beyond me and the great spirit of Poetry; a dream may be a dream still if it wasn't for the faith bestowed upon me by others when I could find none within myself…

To my dear family… my parents, Susan and Ben, and my sister, Sam, and every family member who celebrated my wins as your own and felt the devastation of my every loss as truly as I did myself, your unconditional love and unwavering support, the dedication that you have shown to me and to my every hour spent in the great effort of creating something that I feel is worthy of leaving to Time, has been the foundation of everything I have ever known and loved. Without your grace and understanding, the courage to become what I most desire would have been left unnurtured and unfulfilled. I have become through your care, and it was through your loving words that I found the confidence to share my own. I love you.

To my dear friends… Brooke, Paige, Kenna, Hailey, Sara, and every single one of you who held my hand throughout the years and saw in me something that I had only just begun to discover within myself, thank you. It was your excitement and support that saw me through those dark days of doubt; I could believe for a time in my chosen dream because you all chose to believe in me. My friends, I love you. I am grateful that life has given me such beautiful people in whom I have found the most remarkable of friendships.

To Vela Roth... the brilliance of every star is found in you and your beautiful work. I am humbled by and inspired through the blessing of your friendship. I will forever be grateful to know you. The possibility of publishing was gifted to me by your generous hands, and what this world may know of my work, they will know because of you. I have found the magic of writing through you and your books. You have my gratitude and love, always.

To the readers...what a gift it is for me to have your trust! To have picked up this collection of poetry and dedicated even just a moment of it to your consideration requires your time and belief in what this could be to you; for that faith, you have my gratitude and most sincere appreciation. In your reading, you have met me and shared the vision, for a time, of what I see of the world... I hope that the experience of sharing it with me was as generous and fulfilling as it was for me to share it with you. Thank you for being the glide of my pen and the voice in my head as words were manifested onto the page and thoughts became poetry. Thank you for your time, it is a gift I cherish.

Ad musam aeternam meam...maxima ars umquam nota huic mundo es, et omnem spiritum meum tibi dignum et amans impendo. Semper tuus, semper meus, nos in aeternum.

About the Author

K.P. Alexander is a writer based in Ontario, Canada. Inspired by life, she shares her truth through the written word and creates work that speaks to the gift of existence and the perfect duality of the human experience. She aims to honour the art that the world bestows upon her by feeling it all and turning it into something that she can then give back to the world. When she is not writing, you can find her content in a daydream or deep within the pages of a beloved book. She loves connecting with new people and hopes that you will reach out to her on Instagram or Goodreads at k.p_alexander and on Pinterest at kpalexanderr.